JourneyThrough®

1 Peter

30 Daily Insights from God's Word by **David Burge**

Our Daily Bread Publishing is affiliated
with Our Daily Bread Ministries.

Requests for permission to quote
from this book should be directed to:
Permissions Department
Our Daily Bread Publishing
P.O. Box 3566
Grand Rapids, MI 49501
Or contact us by email at
permissionsdept@dhp.org

Design by Joshua Tan
Typeset by Lidya Jap

ISBN 978-1-913135-34-8

Printed in the United Kingdom
21 22 23 24 25 / 5 4 3 2 1

Foreword

How has your journey with Jesus been so far? Smooth sailing? Full of pain and suffering? Or, perhaps something in between?

Peter writes to assure us that if we're following Jesus, we're on the right track, even if it brings trouble and involves pain. The God of grace is bringing us home, but following Jesus in a fallen world involves many troubles. Knowing this becomes so important when we face trials, such as work or ministry difficulties, and when we endure mental illness or persecution.

If your path is bumpy, and the cross you carry is heavy, keep going! Stand fast! As Christians, we not only see the unseen, but we grow to love someone we've never seen. Peter says of the Lord Jesus, "Though you have not seen him, you love him; and even though you do not see him now, you believe in him and are filled with an inexpressible and glorious joy" (1 Peter 1:8). The Christian's path may be tough, but God gives us joy as we grow to know and love the Lord Jesus. That was Peter's message of encouragement, and it is also the message of this devotional.

Through 1 Peter, God enriches us by clarifying our thinking and strengthening our resolve as we walk with Jesus.

The "God of all grace" (5:10) has much to say to us through 1 Peter, and it is my prayer that wherever this devotional finds you, and at whatever stage of life, it might increase your love and admiration for His glorious Son.

His grateful servant,
David Burge

We're glad you've decided to join us on a journey into a deeper relationship with Jesus Christ!

For over 50 years, we have been known for our daily Bible reading notes, *Our Daily Bread*. Many readers enjoy the pithy, inspiring, and relevant articles that point them to God and the wisdom and promises of His unchanging Word.

Building on the foundation of *Our Daily Bread*, we have developed this devotional series to help believers spend time with God in His Word, book by book. We trust this daily meditation on God's Word will draw you into a closer relationship with Him through our Lord and Saviour, Jesus Christ.

How to use this resource

READ: This book is designed to be read alongside God's Word as you journey with Him. It offers explanatory notes to help you understand the Scriptures in fresh ways.

REFLECT: The questions are designed to help you respond to God and His Word, letting Him change you from the inside out.

RECORD: The space provided allows you to keep a diary of your journey as you record your thoughts and jot down your responses.

An Overview

The Apostle Peter probably wrote 1 Peter in the early 60s AD, around 30 years after Christ's death and resurrection. He mentions the persecution faced by the churches he was addressing, which were spread across Asia Minor (modern-day Turkey) and made up of Jews and Gentiles. We can read examples of persecution in the Book of Acts, but it begins even in the Gospels. Soon after writing 1 and 2 Peter, it seems that Peter may have been crucified like his Lord.

Why would anyone follow Christ when it brought such suffering? Because belonging to Christ is worth any pain that might follow. Peter sets our hearts and minds on the glory and grace that will be ours when Jesus returns.

In this way, 1 Peter is a powerful tonic for the persecuted church, but it helps all of us. It enriches all Christians by pointing us to our true home. It inspires us with God's grace and His glorious plans for us, so that we see the value of pressing on faithfully like His Son. Our increasingly Christlike, holy lives will attract the attention of a watching world, and even if we must suffer undeservedly, God will glorify himself through us and, in a little while, lead us to our eternal home.

The Structure of 1 Peter

1:1–12	God's Blessed People: Glory ahead for God's chosen exiles!
1:13–2:10	God's Holy People: Christians in a watching world
2:11–4:19	God's Meek People: Entrusting ourselves to God while doing good
5:1–14	God's Waiting People: Faithful pastors serving humble flocks

Key Verse

And the God of all grace, who called you to his eternal glory in Christ, after you have suffered a little while, will himself restore you and make you strong, firm and steadfast. —1 Peter 5:10

Day 1

Read 1 Peter 1:1–2

It is common for Christians to feel as though we don't really belong. Some of us have been forcibly removed from our homes because of our faith in Jesus. Others may be living in foreign settings for the sake of the gospel.

In Peter's day, under Emperor Nero, many Christians were persecuted and displaced from their homes. The truth is, all of us, as citizens of heaven, are living in a land to which we don't truly belong. The sin and sadness in our world remind us of this daily. In that sense, all Christians are "exiles, scattered" (1 Peter 1:1), longing for our Promised Land. Just like the character called Christian in John Bunyan's classic book, *The Pilgrim's Progress*, we Christians are pilgrims on our way home.

We may feel saddened by this description, and lament the reality that we, too, are exiles. But for Peter, the sadness of exile is overshadowed by something far greater—he calls Christians "God's elect" (v. 1). God has "chosen" (v. 2) us to be His people! We know this because we have faith in the Lord Jesus (see Ephesians 1:3–6; 2:8–10).

What does it mean to be God's elect? Peter explains in 1 Peter 1:2. He chooses Old Testament sacrifice words ("sanctifying", or making holy, and "sprinkled with his blood"), and New Testament Trinitarian language to help us understand. The persons of God—Father, Son, and Spirit—are each and together responsible for our holy status as God's chosen people. Notice how the *Father* foreknew and chose us, even before the world began; the *Holy Spirit* made us holy or "sanctified" people (definitively when we became Christians, but also progressively day by day); and the *Son* offered His blood so that we enjoy the benefits He purchased on the cross. Reflect on the significance of Jesus' blood sprinkled over you. How might that influence your day?

How conscious are you of the work of the Father, Son, and Spirit, for you? **Our triune God has made a way for us to enjoy these rich realities of "grace and peace", not in small measure, but, as Peter prays, "in abundance" (1 Peter 1:2).** As a Christian, you could speak or even sing these truths to yourself: "I am chosen by my Heavenly Father! His Spirit works mightily in me to obey His Son! Jesus' blood guarantees my holiness!" You may feel far from home in this life, but God tells us through the rest of Peter's letter just how good it is to be one of His chosen, holy people.

ThinkThrough

When you look in the mirror, how much does God's description of you influence the way you see yourself?

How might the portrait of you in these verses change your day?

Day 2

Read 1 Peter 1:3–5

The picture we get of Peter when writing these verses is a man who can hardly contain himself. His desire is to express how richly blessed we are as God's people. He writes from the overflow of his heart. What is it that he is so excited to share?

Peter wants to give credit where credit is due. All praise be to God, whom we now know as our Father through the revealing work of His Son, our Lord Jesus Christ (1 Peter 1:3).

What has God the Father done that is so praiseworthy? Much more than we can yet grasp, and certainly far more than we deserve. The chain of blessings listed in verses 3–5 begins not with our merit, but with the Father's "great mercy" (v. 3) towards us. In mercy, He has given us a "new birth" (v. 3) to become His spiritual children who keenly anticipate the age to come. For this reason, we have "a living hope" (v. 3) that is like a strong rope that joins us with the One who is alive—the resurrected Lord—who has gone before us, who holds onto us, and who promises to return for us.

Our business may fail, people may disappoint us, our finances may be tight, and our health may deteriorate, but as Jesus taught Peter, moths and vermin can't touch our treasure in heaven (Matthew 6:19–20). Our inheritance there "can never perish, spoil or fade" (1 Peter 1:4). Nothing can ruin what God is keeping safe for us (vv. 4–5)!

But what if our faith falters? Maybe we feel we might lose our inheritance. Maybe our anticipation of heaven is lukewarm, and our doubts make heaven seem more like a faint possibility or wish.

God's Word has something far better for us. Our place with Him is not up to us. No—we are *saved* by His grace; we also *persevere* by His grace. Verse 5 assures us it is not our power that will protect us, but God's power. You are "shielded by God's power until the coming of the salvation that is ready to be revealed in the last time" (v. 5).

Our faith is valuable, but we are never called to trust in our faith. Rather, we trust in the God who powerfully saves us. **In His great mercy, His saving of us even includes guarding our faith until He brings us home.**

No wonder Peter overflows with gratitude and praise for God. He knows where he is going and, if you take God at His Word, so do you!

Part of growing as a Christian is learning to stop doubting and to believe what God says about you. How sure are you of your eternal home with the Lord Jesus?

Read the following sentence a few times: "Trusting the God who shields me brings overflowing gratitude and assures me of my eternal inheritance!" How will this assurance change the way you live today?

Day 3

Read 1 Peter 1:6–9

Loyalty, steadfastness, fortitude, grit, resilience, tenderness—such virtues might come to mind when watching an elderly man care for his wife of 50 years who now suffers dementia; a mother still dressing and feeding her 35-year-old son born with a severe disability; or a Christian choosing to be imprisoned, being burnt at the stake, or being wrapped in animal skins and fed to lions by the Romans out of sheer loyalty to Jesus. Faithfulness can be extraordinary to watch, and God calls us to such a life in 1 Peter 1:6–9.

As those who "greatly rejoice" in the undeserved mercy, promises, and protection of God (vv. 3–6), Christians shielded by God's power develop steadfastness, loyalty, and faithfulness under the testing fires of "all kinds of trials" (v. 6).

Remarkably, rejoicing occurs simultaneously with suffering grief (v. 6). We might be tempted to see Christian suffering as meaningless— or worse, a reason to doubt God's care for us. But Peter unveils the good that God is doing through it. In Jesus' life, God brought good out of evil. So what is the good that God achieves through our suffering?

Verse 7 tells us that suffering allows us to see that our faith in Jesus is genuine. A fair-weather friend is one who deserts others when things get uncomfortable, but a genuine friend is one who does not. Even in persecution or hardship, we trust Jesus as Lord. In this way, Christians see something supernatural taking place in our lives—we notice a growing and even surprising resolve given by God to hold fast to Jesus even when it really hurts.

In his letter, Peter urges us to prioritise the imperishable over the perishable. Our refined and tested faith is more resilient than even gold "refined by fire" (v. 7). When we notice how our faith bears costs and refuses to forsake Jesus year after year, we see the authenticity of our faith. Praise God, this is the very faith that joins us to the future blessings of the "praise, glory and honour when Jesus Christ is revealed" (v. 7).

God has transformed us from being those disinterested in the Lord Jesus, to being those who, miraculously, love a Saviour we've never seen. **He transforms us like He transformed Peter—from a fair-weather friend to a committed, faith-demonstrating, trial-enduring disciple.**

Are we to be pitied in our trials? Hardly! For Jesus not only gives us faith and resilience, but also fills us "with an inexpressible and glorious joy, for you are receiving the end result of your faith, the salvation of your souls" (v. 9).

While we aren't called to seek suffering, we need not fear it, either. Suffering for Christ provides a meaningful opportunity—and sometimes a daunting arena—to demonstrate our loyalty to Jesus and to show Him that we love Him.

What opportunities do you have today to show Jesus that you love Him?

In the trials you endure for following Jesus, God wants you to know that these are signs of His saving work, which join you to your eternal inheritance. What could you pray in response to this?

Day 4

Read 1 Peter 1:10–12

One of my earliest memories is visiting the hospital to see my new baby brother. In the hospital corridor was a glass window too high for me to peek through. Straining on my toes, I tried to catch a glimpse of my baby brother sleeping. My father saw my problem and lifted me up so that I could see. How exciting that moment was!

In a similar way, there is excitement in Peter's voice as he describes the way the Old Testament prophets were straining to see more of the Messiah, even as they prophesied about Him.

The prophets realised their message was about God's grace (1 Peter 1:10), the wonderful grace which is a theme running through 1 Peter. Prophets like Isaiah knew God would save through a Messiah (Isaiah 52:13–53:12). The Messiah would suffer and yet be glorified (1 Peter 1:11). But they struggled to know much of the "when" and "exactly how" in the glimpses that God gave them several centuries before the Messiah's arrival.

Now, we are privileged to see clearly what earlier generations were straining to see. We are blessed with not one, but four Gospels which excitedly testify about when and how the Messiah came. The prophets provided the sketch of a Person, but Peter and the other apostles got to see and touch, to know and love, and then to testify about that glorious embodiment of God's grace—the Lord Jesus.

Notice also that Peter says that it was the "Spirit of Christ" (v. 11) who pointed the prophets towards an understanding of Jesus. And it was the same "Holy Spirit" (v. 12) who directed and empowered the apostles' preaching. Both the fulfilment of the prophets' message and the Spirit's revealing work help us to see the certainty and wonder of Scripture. God's ancient promises are wonderfully and divinely met in the life, death, and resurrection of God's Son. **Now we realise all of Scripture was written to help us love and trust God— Father, Son, and Holy Spirit.**

To the people receiving Peter's letter, certainty about Jesus was vital because they were enduring persecution for believing in Him. They needed to be assured of the truth of the gospel. They needed to know their suffering was worth it.

The marvellous news is that this gospel is the true grace of God! So let us stand fast in it (5:12).

Today, as one who has freely received this revelation of God's grace in Jesus, why not let the wonder of God's fulfilled promises and the excitement of His messengers fill your heart!

How might more certainty, clarity, and excitement about the truth of Jesus help you in the challenges you face today?

Day 5

Read 1 Peter 1:13–16

When we come into the world, we have life and breath, but very little knowledge. We are not yet ready to ask: "What is my name? Who are these people around me? What is this place? What are these sights, sounds, and smells?" More profound questions are still years away, such as: "Why am I alive? Does my life have a purpose? How do I know right from wrong when opinions differ? Who is ultimately responsible for my existence?" Sadly, many of our friends will live and die without answers to these essential questions.

How are we Christians to see ourselves? In this second major section in Peter's letter (1 Peter 1:13–2:10), he focuses on our identity as God's holy people in a watching world. Peter wants us to realise who we are. And to do this, the following words are crucial: minds, hope, grace, Jesus' return, children, and holiness.

He begins with our *minds* (1:13), because we live according to what we know. If we think there is no purpose in life, we will live accordingly. But if, like Jesus, our minds are filled with the truths of God's Word, we can expect that abundant fruit will follow.

What does Peter say about our minds? They are to be deliberately "alert" (v. 13). That is, we must live in a state of readiness and be "fully sober" (v. 13) and clear-headed about the things of God. In particular, we are to set our hope on Christ's return (v. 13). Language struggles to express how good it will be for us when Jesus returns. New degrees of God's *grace* will be ours, beginning on that glorious day when Jesus appears to right all wrongs and to take us to our eternal home (v. 13).

God wants that knowledge to sink in for us, and allow it to fill our hearts. May that picture become the way we see ourselves—as *children of God* waiting for Jesus' return (v. 14). **Rather than be intoxicated by worldly ambitions or clouded by the worries of this world, we are to be *holy*. To be holy like our Father is to resemble His purity and His aversion to sin** (vv. 15–16). And we set our hope on the grace to be brought to us when Jesus Christ is revealed at His coming (v. 13).

Such a view of ourselves can't help but transforms our lives. As God's obedient children, we realise our old desires no longer have a place (v. 14). We are grateful to our holy Father who revealed our sin to us, sent His holy Son to pay for it, and welcomes prodigals as His returned children (see Luke 15:11–24). And we joyfully realise we owe ourselves to our holy Father (1 Peter 1:15–16).

In the story of the prodigal son (Luke 15:11–24), imagine if that son had continued with his wild living after he had been so lovingly welcomed back into his father's house. That would be living in the past. So, too, God wants us to realise we are His forgiven, holy children right now. Free to be His, we set our minds and hearts on the things to come.

How might you be an increasingly clear-minded Christian, with your hope set on the grace to come when Jesus returns?

"To be holy like our Father is to resemble His purity and His aversion to sin." How are you becoming more like God in terms of purity of thoughts, words, and deeds? Are you becoming more averse to sin, or more accepting of sin?

Day 6

Read 1 Peter 1:17–21

When we were missionaries in Mongolia, we visited prisons and told precious souls that we had travelled a very long way in order to bring them a message from God. They sensed the message must be of great importance, because our family had moved to their culture and learnt their language in order to share it with them. Out of respect for the effort we had made, Mongolians were willing to hear our message.

Peter uses a similar approach here to motivate us to live as "foreigners" (1 Peter 1:17) in our culture. He tells us to appreciate who God is, and the lengths He has gone to for our sake.

First, who is God to be worthy of loyalty over cultural norms? Peter offers reasons of intimacy and respect. We have an intimate relationship with God as our "Father" (v. 17). Some Christians whose fathers did not show intimacy have testified that knowing God as an intimate father took time to appreciate. At the same time, we respect God for His holiness (v. 16) and role as impartial judge of our lives (v. 17). "Reverent fear" (v. 17) does not mean we are worried that God will forsake us or condemn us, for He will never do that (see Romans 8:1, 39). Rather, it means we remember God is God and treat Him accordingly—with deep awe, trust, and obedience.

Second, to what lengths has God gone for us that motivates our loyalty? Notice the impressive missionary biography of God in 1 Peter 1:18–20. God paid the supreme cost to redeem us from the emptiness of our false religions and ideologies. What was the redeeming price? Peter no doubt remembered vividly the appalling sight of the bleeding, broken body of Jesus on the cross when saying we were ransomed "with the precious blood of Christ, a lamb without blemish or defect" (v. 19).

Remarkably, Jesus' sacrifice was not "Plan B" for God's people. The Son was chosen even "before the creation of the world" (v. 20) for this work, and was revealed recently through His incarnation, death, and resurrection to Peter and others "for your sake" (v. 20).

Since our holy Father has done this for us, let us neither disregard our rescue nor disrespect the great missionary God who has come for us. Let us cheerfully and resolutely see ourselves as His people, and foreigners with good news as we engage with the world. May we, without reluctance, leave our old ways behind in order to adopt the ways of God's holy children.

To what extent have you responded gratefully to God's mission for you in Christ?

What might loyalty to your holy Father look like for you today?

Day 7

Read 1 Peter 1:22–25

We were often asked by friends: "What's it like to live in Mongolia? What are the people like?" We would sometimes answer: "Do you mean Mongolian Christians, or Mongolians generally?" There was often a big difference! Walking into Mongolian Christian gatherings was like walking into a warmer, more loving version of Mongolian culture. There was trust, respect, and love.

Hopefully, in whatever culture you live in, there is an enormous difference between life outside the church and life inside the church. That is also what Peter expected when writing these verses.

He calls Christians those who have "purified yourselves by obeying the truth so that you have sincere love for each other" (1 Peter 1:22). I've never lived in a culture where "sincere love for each other" is normal. But I have lived in church families like that. Yes, the love is always imperfect, but it can be sincere.

Sincere love is a good start, but Peter would have our love get richer still. He adds: "Love one another deeply, from the heart" (v. 22). We are to look at each other and see people worth loving, deeply. We are all different shapes and sizes, and come from different cultures. The world teaches us to put each other into categories such as pretty or ugly, fit or overweight, independent or needy, influential or inconsequential. But these are shallow, temporary ways of viewing eternal souls. **We must learn to see ourselves and each other as precious souls brought to immortality through God's Word (v. 23).**

The temporary is often contrasted with the imperishable in 1 Peter, and we Christians share in God's imperishable life by receiving God's "living and enduring word" (v. 23). To make his point, Peter excitedly quotes Isaiah's ancient yet living promises (from Isaiah 40:6–8): although humans are frail and will die, God's Word, which promises to save a people for himself, stands forever. We are His people, made imperishable by the gospel of Jesus which the apostles announced (1 Peter 1:12, 23).

It is not as though the church has to generate love from within. Rather, we are God's born-again, Spirit-enlivened people. The Spirit enables us to love, which is the chief Christian virtue. With the Spirit, we have the wellspring of God's love within; each day God gives us is our opportunity to live that love out.

Think of the Christians you spend most time with—perhaps a spouse, relatives, or friends. What would it look like for you to love them more sincerely, deeply, and from the heart?

What kind of loving words and actions would they appreciate from you?

Day 8

Read 1 Peter 2:1–3

Today's verses provide a simple yet vitally important message to spiritual children of all ages. The contrast is memorable and the language is strong. Peter says "rid yourselves" (1 Peter 2:1) of evil that does not belong in God's children. At the same time, learn to "crave" (v. 2)—with the desperate appetite of a newborn baby—what is pure and wholesome (see Psalm 34:8). It's a simple message that, if heeded, will transform our lives.

Five harmful traits are identified for us to eliminate from our lives (v. 1). It would be well worth pausing after each word in order to detect traces of them in our hearts, minds, wills, or actions.

First, "malice" can mean ill will, wickedness, badness, depravity, or evil. As confronting as this might be, are there any parts of your life that God brings to your conscience?

Second, "deceit", or guile, refers to deceiving others with an impression that is not genuine. Selfish motives or critical judgments of others are things we tend to cover up with deceit. Removing deceit makes us more trustworthy.

Third, "hypocrisy" refers similarly to having a double life or second face—when the public self and the true self are not one. Jesus' instruction for overcoming hypocrisy is to live before an audience of One—that is, our Father in heaven, who sees what we do in secret as well as in public (see Matthew 6:1–18).

Fourth, "envy" is the awful response of jealousy or resentment towards others. If we are not content with what we have, and if we do not love others enough to rejoice at their prosperity, miserable envy follows. Envy leads us to despise those who have what we want, exposing our lack of love. Who are the people you envy? Could you thank God now for them instead?

Fifth, Peter wants us to work on eliminating all false or evil speech, including "slander", which is to defame or speak untruthfully against someone.

We are to grow in our distaste for traits we may have been tolerating for many years.

What was perhaps sweet in the past takes on a bitterness now, and we begin to develop a different appetite. We might find ourselves speaking of some topics less, and other topics more, and all with a new, gracious tone.

Let's imitate the desperate newborn baby (1 Peter 2:2). Our new milk is God's Word (see 1:23, 25), which nourishes our new and imperishable lives.

ThinkThrough

What are the occasions you hear yourself thinking, "I probably shouldn't say this, but . . . "? Ask God to help you rid yourself of harmful speech.

How can you be like an adult "baby" who craves God's Word and delights in the goodness of God?

Day 9

Read 1 Peter 2:4–5

Many masterpieces begin with a sketch. Throughout the unfolding story of Scripture, God provides sketch after sketch relating particularly to Jesus' first and second coming.

In Isaiah 28, God provides a beautiful sketch of the rebuilding of Jerusalem. It is no small renovation. For His dwelling, and for the dwelling of His people, God is going to start again from the very foundation stone (Isaiah 28:16). Unlike any ordinary man-made city, this new city is constructed by God to be a holy, eternal city where justice and righteousness triumph over human corruption and evil (v. 17).

So far, Peter has been talking about Christians being holy as God is holy, but now we zoom out to see the bigger picture. God is building something new with Jesus as the cornerstone—the first and foundational one.

This city that God is building is no mere rebuild of Jerusalem and an earthly temple. Rather, God is dwelling more intimately and permanently in us. Peter says in verses 4–5: "As you come to him, the living Stone—rejected by humans but chosen by God and precious to him—you also, like living stones, are being built into a spiritual house."

God's view of the church is more than a spectacular new temple in which He dwells; God's church is made up of God's people.

God's people are also the new holy priests for that temple. The sacrifices of rams and goats are replaced by the spiritual sacrifices of our whole lives offered to God through Jesus Christ (see also Hebrews 13:15–16; Romans 12:1–2). The old covenant language of what is pleasing to God in temples, priests, and sacrifices is now applied to Christ and His holy people. Christ, and we in Him, become the temple and priests whose holy lives and good deeds become the sacrifices God enjoys (see John 2:19–21; 1 Corinthians 6:18–20).

There is a lot going on in this image for us to appreciate. It shows the wonder of God's plans in Israel's history, rituals, and promises so that we can comprehend what God is doing through Christ and Christ's people. Even before creation, God had planned to make an eternal people to dwell with Him.

The heartbeat of Scripture is God's determination that "I will be their God, and they will be my people" (Jeremiah 31:33; Revelation 21:7).

By giving us the images of temple and priest, and then fulfilling them in us, God gives us another way to understand His glorious eternal purposes being accomplished.

Reflect on the ways that Old Testament history helps us to appreciate Jesus. What examples can you think of?

It may encourage you to know your significance as a Christian is far bigger than being an individual child of God. You are part of something much bigger, and at the centre of His timeless plans for the world! Spend some time now to meditate on this vision of God's spiritual house and your place in it, and give thanks.

Read 1 Peter 2:6–8

A friend of mine told me that Jesus did not expect to be crucified. Rather, my friend thinks, Jesus accidentally pushed the religious leaders too far and died against His will.

But this is not what the Gospels teach, nor what the rest of Scripture teaches, even as far back as the book of Genesis. God's enemies *never* take Him by surprise. We know the opposition we face never surprises God, either (see Genesis 3:15).

Each verse in today's reading cites a different Old Testament text. The string of quotations begins with the phrase, "For in Scripture it says" (1 Peter 2:6). Peter does not think of Scripture as an old, dusty history book, but as the ever-living Word of God, relevant for the here and now (see 1 Peter 1:23). God still speaks through words He inspired many centuries earlier—in Peter's day, and so, too, in ours. When you read any part of Scripture, such as the Psalms or 1 Peter, do you realise God is addressing you in your "now"?

What, then, are the ancient-yet-fresh Scriptures saying to us now? God is describing two types of people in relation to Jesus, who is God's "chosen and precious cornerstone" (2:6). The first type of person is "the one who trusts in him" and who "will never be put to shame" (v. 6). The one who acknowledges the Lord Jesus will be spared the destructive judgment coming to the arrogant who do not accept God's Word (see Isaiah 28:14–22).

The second type of person God addresses is "those who do not believe" (1 Peter 2:7). Peter uses Psalm 118:22 to warn them about the terrible mistake of misjudging God's servants and plans. The world's rejection of Jesus is no reason to distrust God's Word, but to trust it all the more, because it even foretells His rejection (1 Peter 2:8).

God's people in Isaiah's day, Peter's day, and our day, are reminded that though the world offers us an alternative that seems to be stronger or more blessed than Jesus, we must not be fooled. Our Lord, the suffering servant and man of sorrows, is Immanuel, the glorious Son of God with us.

Since we are God's chosen and elect people, our trust in Jesus was foreordained, as we saw in 1 Peter 1:1–3. But the rejection of Jesus was also foreordained—"which is also what they were destined for" (2:8). Peter realised that Judas Iscariot, for example, was destined to betray Jesus (Acts 1:20), as well as "both Herod and Pontius Pilate, along with the Gentiles and the peoples of Israel" (4:27–28 ESV; see Romans 9:22).

Nothing takes God by surprise— including the evil plan to kill the Lamb of God and to harm or mock His children. Trust in God is always well-placed, even when living for Him really hurts.

How might you be tempted to forsake Jesus for the comforts that come from the world, or because of the world's pressures? What can you do to resist?

Reflect on Jesus as the "chosen and precious cornerstone" (1 Peter 2:6). What does it mean, and how will it impact the way you live today?

Day 11

Read 1 Peter 2:9–10

The New Testament urges Christians to encourage one another—to speak truths to each other that strengthen and give courage. It's a shame when people feel so despondent or self-critical that they give up on a relationship or a ministry because of despair. If only we were more encouraged and more encouraging of one another. Can you think of times someone encouraged you in your faith or ministry? What effect did it have?

Today's passage is God's way of encouraging you. In 1 Peter 2:9, he says four things for you to cling to, each using Old Testament descriptions that are loaded with significance.

First, "you are a chosen people". Just as God chose Israel from among the nations, God chose you to be His and He is committed to you forever (see Hebrews 13:5).

Second, you are "a royal priesthood". In Peter's day, kings and priests were privileged with special roles of service to God. Now, God gives you a share in the kingdom work of Jesus our King and Mediator.

Third, you are a "holy nation". The nation of Israel was set apart to represent God in the watching world. Israel failed in her task, and our representation of God is still far from perfect, but in Christ we are set apart for this privileged role. Day by day, you are being made holy through the inner working of the Holy Spirit.

Fourth, God says that you are His "special possession". Incredibly, even though God does not need anyone or anything, He says over and over through Scripture that He loves and delights in us (see Zephaniah 3:14–20). May His love overwhelm your minds and hearts! You have a special place in God's heart.

Such truths are intended to fill you with overflowing gratitude and cause you to "declare the praises of him who called you out of darkness into his wonderful light" (1 Peter 2:9).

Whatever your work or life situation might be, God gives you a fulfilling purpose—you are to allow your heart's gratitude to overflow to the world and to share how merciful God is to have brought you from darkness to light (v. 10).

ThinkThrough

God wants you and your church to know who you are to Him. Read in 1 Peter 2:9–10 again. What strikes you most from these descriptions of you?

How might you let these truths fill your heart and overflow into praise of God today?

Day 12

Read 1 Peter 2:11–12

Have you ever lost your voice? Sometimes, those who have lost their voice may resort to scribbling on a notepad or communicating with hand gestures, until their voice returns.

The persecuted Christians in Peter's day probably didn't have much of a voice in their society. So Peter emphasises the importance of their actions, which will speak for them while they suffer unjustly. God works through injustice to present the gospel through His meek and faithful people.

These verses introduce the third major section in Peter's letter. Now that we know how much we mean to God as His holy people (1 Peter 1:13–2:10), we are ready to live boldly in a world that may dislike us and seek to hurt us. For this reason, the next section (2:11–4:19) could be called "God's Meek People: Entrusting Ourselves to God While Doing Good".

In today's reading, Peter says that until Jesus returns, God's special people are living as "foreigners and exiles" (2:11) in the world, a land that is not our own. Our citizenship in heaven means we don't always fit in well on earth. For now, we remain separated physically from our great King and our promised land, and we live among unbelievers who

sometimes falsely accuse Christians of wrongdoing (v. 12).

Peter guides Christians by telling us what to avoid and what to seek. First, we must "abstain from sinful desires" (v. 11) or desires of the flesh, because these fleshly desires "wage war" against our souls. Our souls are the more essential and permanent selves which live on when our bodies fail. In 2 Peter 1:13–14, Peter describes death as leaving the "tent" of his body. Desires of the flesh might include a pull towards pornography, wealth, prestige, selfish ambition, or indulging our stomachs with food and drinks. **As foreigners and exiles in the world, we should no longer be mastered by these desires, but instead follow Jesus as Lord, whose ways lead to life.**

Peter promotes "good lives" and "good deeds" (1 Peter 2:12). Such living is not only good for our souls, but also points the watching world towards the God we follow. He says some will come to Christ through our witness (v. 12). In this way, Peter echoes Jesus' teaching from the Sermon on the Mount, when He says "you are the light of the world", and that through your good deeds, people will "glorify your Father in heaven" (Matthew 5:16).

_____

_____

_____

_____

_____

_____

_____

_____

_____

_____

_____

_____

_____

_____

_____

_____

_____

_____

_____

Who are some unbelieving friends who seem particularly interested in how you live as a Christian? Are your deeds and actions pointing them towards God?

What are some desires of the flesh that seem to master you, and how might you allow good deeds to take their place?

Day 13

Read 1 Peter 2:13–17

As a father of four children, I have taught each of them that it often takes more strength to do right than it does to do wrong. It can be very hard to forgive and be kind when our strong desire is to hold a grudge or to act selfishly.

Meekness requires the strength of being submissive and humble, which was modelled by Jesus (Matthew 5:5; see Philippians 2:6–8). **Christians can submit themselves to others because we know it is ultimately God, not the people with authority or power over us, who truly governs everything.** Peter repeatedly calls Christians to meekness—to "submit yourselves" (1 Peter 2:13, 18; 3:1); to be "compassionate and humble" (3:8); and to be those who may "suffer for doing good" (3:17).

Peter gives examples of how this applies to four spheres of authority under which Christians may struggle: governors or emperors (2:13–17); masters (2:18–20); husbands (3:1–7); and lastly, meekness towards one another and towards the world in general (3:8–4:11).

Peter begins with the instruction to submit to "every human authority" (2:13) and mentions the emperor and the governors who rule. Why do we submit to human authorities? Peter says it is "for the Lord's sake" (v. 13). Human rulers are "sent by him to punish those who do wrong and to commend those who do right" (v. 14).

God created us to be relational beings who form communities. He sets governing authorities to prevent anarchy that comes when people do whatever they want. Our allegiance to God does not mean we ignore these means of social order; instead, we must gratefully recognise their authority (see Paul's similar instruction in Romans 13:1–7).

Christians live under the lordship of Jesus, but this is never to be an excuse for breaking civil laws, such as avoiding taxes or embezzling funds or resources from work. Such behaviour dishonours the Lord and gives unbelievers reason to condemn the way of Christ—this would be using our freedom "as a cover-up for evil" (1 Peter 2:16).

If we do good in society's eyes, and together form a reputation for being upstanding citizens, our record will serve to "silence the ignorant talk of foolish people" (v. 15) who may accuse Christians of various evils. Historically, Christians have been used mightily by God for the flourishing of society, not by avoiding the world, but by serving it in Christ's name.

Some governing authorities are faithful in their service of people, and others less so. The emperors and governors in Peter's day were often tyrannical and unjust. And yet Peter points to their God-given authority and the need to submit to them as long as they do not demand disobedience to Christ (see Acts 4:18–21; 5:29).

He concludes with a most helpful summary, which would be valuable to memorise: "Show proper respect to everyone, love the family of believers, fear God, honour the emperor" (1 Peter 2:17).

What are some things you can thank God for in the way your national or local authorities govern?

How might you honour someone you expect to relate with today?

Day 14

Read 1 Peter 2:18–20

Most people live with some kind of fear. We might fear that we will lose our job, or that we won't have enough money. We might fear a broken marriage or perhaps a life of singleness. Some of us worry about our children's future or what people think of us. Or we fear embarrassment and shame.

The good news for Christians is that when we trust and fear God, we need not live in fear of people, bad situations, or threats of any kind (see Genesis 15:1; Exodus 14:13; Deuteronomy 31:7–8). When Jesus' disciples worry or are afraid, He urges them to trust their Father who cares for them (Matthew 6:30–31). As Christians, we can confidently say: "The Lord is my helper; I will not be afraid; what can mere mortals do to me?" (Hebrews 13:6).

Fearing God has been a theme in 1 Peter (as we saw in 1:17 and 2:17), and it continues into today's reading. In verse 17, Peter urged the church to fear God; in verse 18, he now urges slaves to submit to their masters "in reverent fear of God", or "with all respect" (v. 18 ESV). If they fear God and are "conscious of God" (v. 19), they can submit to their masters more easily.

So what does it mean to fear God and be conscious of God? You may be familiar with this phrase from Proverbs 9:10: "The fear of the LORD is the beginning of wisdom." It describes a posture before God that is full of awe, reverence, faith, and that recognises our weakness and unworthiness as creatures before our majestic and holy God.

Some servants in Peter's time were loved by their masters, but others were terribly mistreated. For the mistreated, Peter's words would have been difficult to accept. **But with this awe and reverence for God, Christians can submit to all kinds of temporary hardship, knowing that our lives are in His good, eternal hands.**

In 1 Peter 2:18, Peter includes not only the gentle masters, but also "those who are harsh". God sees and knows what we are enduring, and He also knows our hearts trust Him while we endure it. When we endure because we are "conscious of God" (v. 19), God calls it a commendable thing (vv. 19–20), or more literally, "a gracious thing" (ESV).

As Christians, we might be prepared to submit to God's will, but we may not be so ready to submit to the demands of people, particularly if their treatment of us is not kind or fair. But we know that through our service to all kinds of masters, we are always serving God and showing Him that we fear Him. It's comforting to know that God notices this, and calls it commendable—a gracious thing.

How might you show grace in your response to some of the demands placed upon you?

Are there situations in which you might advise a Christian friend to consider a different employer or to seek relief from a crushing situation?

Day 15

Read 1 Peter 2:21–23

Sometimes, parents need to prepare their child to go through painful things. For instance, they may have to explain to their child that a doctor will need to remove a limb or do a skin graft. With this letter, Peter is likewise preparing his loved ones for suffering.

Peter understands that when he instructs servants to submit to their masters (1 Peter 2:18–20), and wives to submit to their own husbands (3:1–6), he may be asking no easy thing. In today's passage, Peter therefore provides further reasons to help Christians understand the importance of submission. We saw in previous days that we submit to others for the Lord's sake, out of reverence for Him, and because it is a gracious thing in God's sight.

Today, we see that submission also makes us more like the Lord Jesus!

We are called to this submission "because Christ suffered for you, leaving you an example, that you should follow in his steps" (2:21). **We follow the footsteps of One who suffered for us. His suffering was not only to save us, but was also the model of a godly life.**

In verses 22 to 23, Peter describes Jesus the suffering servant using the words of Isaiah 53:7 and 9 to make his point. Jesus' suffering was neither deserved nor fair—He was sinless and without deceit. And when mistreated, He neither retaliated nor threatened His oppressors. How could Jesus do that? How could He relinquish His right to demand better treatment?

Verse 23 provides the impressive answer: it was because "he entrusted himself to him who judges justly". Jesus knew His life was in God's sovereign hands. He trusted God enough to trust His Father's justice, even while enduring the bitter injustice of a world that spurns its Creator and Saviour.

In today's news we often see constant retaliatory fighting between political and religious groups. Insults and bombs are thrown in response to insults and bombs coming the other way. But Jesus' disciples are to be like their Master, who told Peter to put his sword away (Matthew 26:52), and to respond to persecutors with the opposite spirit (5:43–45).

Remarkably, Christians love and pray for their enemies! With Jesus' life within us, we can even rejoice and consider ourselves blessed when people persecute us for bearing Jesus' name (v. 10). Through our

suffering, we more closely resemble the One who
so kindly suffered for us.

_____

_____

_____

_____

_____

_____

Life can feel unfair,
disappointing, or
just out of control.
In what situations
might you imitate
Jesus by entrusting
yourself to Him who
judges justly?

What changes might
that require of you,
and how might
you draw strength
from God and His
people?

_____

_____

_____

_____

_____

_____

_____

_____

_____

_____

_____

Day 16

Read 1 Peter 2:24–25

When I was a teenager, I wondered why we sang and talked about Jesus' death at church, week after week. I wondered, "Doesn't it make God sad that we keep talking about His Son's death? Isn't it a sad and negative event that we shouldn't dwell on too much?" It was only later, that I began to understand how important Jesus' death is. Indeed, Paul summarised his message and ministry as: "We preach Christ crucified" (1 Corinthians 1:23).

In today's verses, Peter helps us to appreciate Jesus' death for three reasons: His death is substitutionary, enlivening, and restorative.

First, Jesus' suffering is substitutionary. Peter's words are disturbingly graphic: "He himself bore our sins in his body on the cross" (1 Peter 2:24). The contrast between what Jesus contributes and what we contribute is stark. What we bring to the cross is our sin; what Jesus does on the cross is to bear our sin in His body, to suffer the wrath of God that we deserved.

Before we reject the idea of enduring unjust suffering ourselves, we must realise that we needed Jesus' unjust suffering for us. We need grace to triumph over fairness. We benefit first from that which we then learn to do.

Second, Jesus' suffering is enlivening. Not only does He bear the guilt and shame of our sin, He also removes its power over us. Jesus intended that we reorient our lives away from the sin that He dealt with—we "die to sins" (v. 24)—in order that we can begin to "live for righteousness" (v. 24). By His wounds we are not only forgiven, but also healed—freed from the curse and power of sin. If we have been Christians for many years, we may have forgotten what it was like to be enslaved to sin and disinterested in God's righteousness. Let's be reminded today that God has given us a new life that chooses His righteous ways day by day.

Third, it is restorative. Peter explains, "now you have returned to the Shepherd and Overseer of your souls" (v. 25). The God who created us has, in the person of His Son, restored us to himself. When we come to the Lord Jesus, we come to the good shepherd of Psalm 23. The Lord mercifully "lays down his life for the sheep" (John 10:11). Our triune God is the Shepherd and Overseer of our souls.

Early Christian theologian Augustine of Hippo said: "You have made us for yourself, and our hearts are restless until they rest in you." Our bodies might be burned at the stake or thrown to lions, but thanks be to God, we never leave the constant care of the Overseer of our souls.

ThinkThrough

Peter saw with his own eyes the day when Jesus bore our sins in His body on the cross. He shares that memory with you so that you will visualise it, too. Why not spend some time now visualising what Peter describes?

What does that image stir up within you? How might that encourage you to live differently?

Day 17

Read 1 Peter 3:1–2

I cannot ice-skate well, so awe fills me whenever I watch ice-skating pairs move so effortlessly and beautifully across the ice during the Winter Olympics. Usually, the man is tall, strong, and often in dark clothing that draws little attention. His partner, the woman, is typically smaller, lighter, and dressed in bright, flowing clothing. They are distinct from each other, yet their differences make their routine all the more beautiful.

Marriage between a man and a woman is intended to similarly benefit from difference and harmony. Many who come to Christ from different cultures want to know: What does a Christian marriage look like?

On the basis of God's good design (see Genesis 1:27), He intended husbands to lovingly lead, and wives to be respectful of their husband's leading as they live in union.

It is important for husbands to notice in 1 Peter 3:1 that Peter does not tell husbands to force submission upon their wives. Rather, he appeals with gentleness to wives to voluntarily *submit yourselves* to your own husbands". This submission is not to every man or husband, but to "your own" husband (v. 1)—the one who is to be sacrificially and lovingly committed to your welfare. This is part of living with "purity and reverence" before God (v. 2, or literally "fear of God", as we saw in 1 Peter 2:18).

Tragically, many husbands mistreat the precious woman who entrusts herself to his care. Peter will address husbands in 3:7.

Today's verses are aimed at a different though sometimes related problem of a wife resisting her husband's role to lead, making his leadership more difficult. Many husbands are ridiculed, dishonoured, and despised by their wives, sometimes in front of their children or even publicly.

Men, who by nature deeply value respect and will die for honour, find such home environments extremely difficult. They often retaliate by escaping home responsibilities or failing to love the wife they promised to love. This is not an excuse for men, but it is one reason Scripture urges wives to submit themselves to their husbands. A male ice-skater can't effectively lead a partner who is resistant to his leading.

Another reason is also given which ties in with the "watching world" theme of 1 Peter. **Some unbelieving husbands in Peter's day were so struck**

by their Christian wife's meekness, purity, and reverence for God that they, without words, were drawn to the One who transformed their wife.

I know of a town where many husbands were alcoholics. They wasted money, were lazy, and were not good husbands or fathers, and their wives found little in them to respect. But when an older Christian woman urged the wives to try to treat their husbands with respect rather than their usual scorn, a number of the men followed the script of 1 Peter 3:1–2. Some husbands started coming to church and to faith in Christ. Gradually, they became loving and responsible leaders of their families. They were intrigued and eventually won over by the meekness and grace of their wives.

Submission to your own husband, purity, and reverence for God—what do these features look like for you if you are a wife?

For others, whether single or married, how does this model for wives inspire you to support wives and to imitate their trust in Jesus?

Day 18

Different cultures value different traits for men and women. In Mongolia where my family once lived, humility is a highly esteemed trait for women, according to tradition. Other cultures might esteem beauty, intelligence, or education. What are the traits our Creator calls women and wives to pursue?

1 Peter 3:3–4 provides helpful answers. The beauty industry may be responsible for some of the unhealthy pressure that women feel to be outwardly beautiful. In Peter's day, the expectations included "outward adornment, such as elaborate hairstyles and the wearing of gold jewellery or fine clothes" (v. 3). But again, what sort of beauty does God admire? Verse 4 reveals it is "your inner self, the unfading (literally, "imperishable") beauty of a gentle and quiet spirit, which is of great worth in God's sight" (v. 4).

What is a gentle and quiet spirit? First, "gentle" can also be translated as "meek" and is the opposite of being harsh or tyrannical. It is a trait that both men and women are to pursue, since it is used to describe Jesus who is "gentle and humble in heart" (Matthew 11:29). Though our world might reward self-assertiveness and even ruthlessness, gentleness is a wonderfully disarming trait of mature Christians. Gentle people are safe to approach, and a wife's gentleness contributes much to marital harmony.

Second, "quiet" refers to a tranquil, peaceful existence or attitude, as one who is at rest (see 1 Timothy 2:2; 1 Thessalonians 4:11). To lack quietness could mean being disturbed, reactive, and frightened, which is to forget God's calming sovereignty. God's intention is that wives "not give way to fear" (1 Peter 3:6). It can be scary for a woman to submit to a husband. As one woman shared, "If I was afraid my husband will take advantage of my submission, I might react by resisting his leadership and fighting for my rights." Fear makes submission much harder.

Peter seems to be thinking of this gentle and quiet spirit within the context of marriage, in particular. He mentions in verse 5 the "holy women of the past", including Sarah, who submitted to their husbands. Sarah called Abraham her "lord" (Genesis 18:12). Perhaps with Sarah's culture in mind, Peter does not say that Christian wives should do the same today. Yet the principle of submission to one's husband, however it might look in your culture and time, is to be the enduring attribute of Christian wives.

A gentle and quiet spirit fits with Peter's overall promotion of lives that are sober-minded and meek. Our lives and marriages are enriched by the knowledge that the Lord is in control of all things.

How might you, as a man or woman, have given too much attention to outward appearances?

How might a more beautiful inner self become a greater pursuit for you?

Read 1 Peter 3:7

Near our front door at home, we have a wedding photo. When I look at my wife in that photo, I am filled with a sense of wonder that she would entrust herself and so much of her future happiness to me. When a bride says "I do", it is an incredible honour for a man to receive.

But tragically, a husband may forget or even deliberately trample on the honour and trust given him by his wife. It must grieve God to see a precious daughter mistreated by the man who should be most committed to her flourishing.

In 1 Peter 3:1 and 7, Peter uses the phrase "in the same way" to link what he says here to husbands and wives, with the way all of us are to submit to authorities (2:13, 18; 3:8) and to imitate Jesus (see 3:13–18).

God gives two instructions to guide husbands. First, "be considerate as you live with your wives" (v. 7). The word "considerate" is literally "according to knowledge" or "in an understanding way". What is this knowledge? Is it knowledge of God, or knowledge of women more generally, or knowledge of one's wife in particular? It is probably all of these. Living according to knowledge is to live wisely with your wife.

Peter refers to the wife as "the weaker vessel" (v. 7 ESV). The word "vessel" suggests that it may be her body and physical strength he is primarily referring to. Certainly, Peter is not suggesting less intelligence, wisdom, or capability, as some Christians have wrongly thought at different times.

Being physically weaker can put wives in a vulnerable position in marriage. Is this a reason for a husband to disrespect one's wife? On the contrary, Peter adds a second instruction that is the opposite of abuse or degradation. Husbands are to "treat them with respect" (v. 7), or more literally, to "grant her honour". Many wives appreciate having an understanding husband—one who honours her and respects the ways her needs and desires may differ from his.

The honour due to every Christian wife comes not only through her created dignity as a human, but also as God's child. Wives are "heirs with you of the gracious gift of life" (v. 7), and are never to be treated with less respect than a fellow heir of this gift. A wife is to be cherished as a child of the King and as a dear sister in Christ.

A further motivation Peter adds is "so that nothing will hinder your prayers" (v. 7). This may refer primarily to the husbands' prayers, since God's ears are open to the prayers of the righteous (v. 12). A cruel or degrading husband should not presume to have God's ear. Such a husband will also struggle to pray with his wife, and so miss the marital strengthening that praying together brings.

How might you or your church better promote a healthy view of manhood and womanhood?

How might you or your church promote healthy marriages?

Day 20

Read 1 Peter 3:8–12

In political, business, military, sporting, and many other spheres, pressure can have fascinating effects. In winning teams, pressure brings players closer together as they work harder for each other. In losing teams, pressure exposes disunity and magnifies little strains until the team becomes its own worst enemy.

Peter is writing to Christians who are facing all kinds of pressure in their lives for Christ. Here, he begins 1 Peter 3:8 with the word "finally". Having addressed the way Christians are to live under government authorities (2:13–17), human masters (2:18–25), and within marriage (3:1–7), he has a final general appeal to whole churches ("all of you", 3:8) about how we are to stick together, especially when under pressure.

We are to have what we might call meekness traits: "be like-minded, be sympathetic, love one another, be compassionate and humble" (v. 8). Here are some possible symptoms that arise when we lack these traits: finding pleasure in controversy and disputes; showing little interest in the feelings and hardships of others; being known as a driven person because of your commitment to personal ambitions; preferring to talk and give advice in a conversation, rather than to listen or to ask for advice. Do any of these describe you?

As a Christian community, the traits in verse 8 are to be modelled and nurtured by pastors and leaders as we make disciples of Jesus.

We are to be like Jesus towards one another. When we enjoy strong fellowship among Christians, we will be in a stronger position to face the outside pressures of insults and evil (v. 9), and to bless those who mistreat us. When we follow God's way, we inherit a blessing (v. 9). Under God, the future is bleak for those who do evil, but His eternal prosperity comes to those who trust and follow Him.

Peter urges us to imitate Christ, using the words of Psalm 34, in the areas of speech (1 Peter 3:10), doing good (v. 11), pursuing peace (v. 11), and living prayerful lives (v. 12).

The citation of Psalm 34 reminds us that this is not a new challenge. To be God's loyal children has never been easy, but it has always been, and forever will be, the path of ultimate blessing.

When you hear Peter's words, "be like-minded, be sympathetic, love one another, be compassionate and humble" (1 Peter 3:8), which trait do you find easiest, and which do you find hardest? Why?

God's Spirit helps us to grow in these areas. How will you cooperate with the Spirit in pursuing these changes today?

Day 21

Read 1 Peter 3:13–17

Not all suffering is unjust—sometimes we make a mistake and suffer the consequences. We drop the milk and have to clean it up, or we falsely accuse someone and receive an angry response. So, too, with persecution; sometimes Christians suffer because we have been irritating or arrogant. **But in today's verses, Peter says that if we must suffer hostility from others, let's make sure it is only for doing good.**

In the previous verses, Peter said that generally, believers' desire to live peacefully and to do good would lead to stronger relationships and various blessings (see also Psalm 1). This general truth is expressed in the next question he asks: "Who is going to harm you if you are eager to do good?" (1 Peter 3:13). Normally, though not always, kindness meets a good response.

But when suffering comes *undeservedly*, Peter doesn't want us to be unsettled. He says that sometimes suffering will be completely unjust, yet this does not threaten God's promised blessing (v. 14). Why, then, can we face suffering confidently? Peter gives two reasons.

First, God's children have nothing to fear! As we mature as Christians, we realise that we need not fear—and we must not fear—people or things (as we saw also in v. 6). The only space for fear in our lives is in the form of a loving reverence for God. In the words of verse 15, we "revere Christ as Lord".

In your life as a Christian, are you afraid of people or consequences that might come if you lovingly, faithfully serve Christ? God says: "Do not fear their threats; do not be frightened" (v. 14).

Second, we can endure suffering confidently because it leads to opportunities to share Jesus with others. Peter tells us to "be prepared to give an answer to everyone who asks you to give the reason for the hope that you have" (v. 15).

Even here, with the opportunity to share our hope, we remain gentle and respectful, and act according to a good conscience (vv. 15–16). That way, if another round of suffering follows, the attack is more obviously shameful and undeserved. So if we must suffer, says Peter, let it be for doing good as we follow Christ.

ThinkThrough

What fears make you feel like giving up doing what you think is right?

Ask God to forgive you for the times you have distrusted His care. Say to Him, "Lord, help me to fear no person or thing."

Day 22

Read 1 Peter 3:18–22

In many sports, if players are injured or exhausted, they can call for a substitute. A substitute takes our place and gives us relief.

Jesus endured suffering not only to be our encouraging model, but also to be our substitute. His unjust suffering was central to God's plan that His Son would be "the righteous for the unrighteous" (1 Peter 3:18). He is the sacrificial lamb, the substitute for sinners from God (see Isaiah 53:3–6). Stuck in sin, we needed Christ to suffer in our place as our sin-bearing substitute. Jesus "suffered once for sins" that He did not commit, "to bring you to God" (1 Peter 3:18).

For Jesus, this unjust suffering ended well. Though He died undeservedly, He was "made alive" (v. 19). Undoubtedly, unjust suffering will end well for those who are joined to Christ by faith.

This truth leads to one of the most difficult texts to understand in the New Testament—1 Peter 3:19–22. There is a relationship between physical events and spiritual realities, and Peter seems to be drawing comparisons between the church's situation and Noah's on two points.

First, Peter appears to be saying that after His resurrection, Jesus went to proclaim His victory over the same spiritual beings who were opposed to God in Noah's day (vv. 19–20, see also 2 Peter 2:4–5).

Paul similarly describes the spiritual powers at play in our world when he says: "Our struggle is not against flesh and blood, but against the rulers, against the authorities, against the powers of this dark world and against the spiritual forces of evil in the heavenly realms" (Ephesians 6:12). God's servants are victorious in Jesus, whose victory is felt even by God's ancient spiritual enemies.

Second, Noah was preserved on the day of God's judgment with water—water which both judged and cleansed. Similarly, for us, the water from the flood "symbolises baptism that now saves you also" (1 Peter 3:21). Baptism reminds us that Christ's physical, substitutionary death (v. 18) has spiritual, cleansing power.

We can be certain of Jesus' victory for us as physical and spiritual beings, and have a clear conscience before God, because of Jesus' resurrection (v. 21)—"he was put to death in the body but made alive in the Spirit" (v. 18). We can know, as Noah did, that we are God's saved people because of these physical events with spiritual significance.

In verse 22, we are shown a vision of the glorious place that Jesus now enjoys at God's right hand. The humbled one has been wonderfully exalted—Jesus submitted to suffering and death, but now, angels, authorities, and powers submit to Him.

ThinkThrough

Jesus, our righteous substitute, is no longer dead but is wonderfully alive. His victory over the spiritual realm is our victory, too. How might you respond to these truths?

In many cultures, belief in the spiritual world generates fear and many rituals. In other cultures, disbelief in the spiritual world leads to complacency about the spirits. How can Christians walk a healthy path between these two responses?

Day 23

Read 1 Peter 4:1–6

Having explained in 1 Peter 3:18–22 that Jesus himself suffered unjustly while being obedient to God, even to death, Peter now exhorts Christians to arm themselves with that same resolve, so that they, too, might live victoriously. In doing this, he gives three motivations to resist sin and follow Christ's way. The motivations follow the words "therefore" (4:1), "for" (v. 3), and "but" (v. 5).

First, Peter urges, "therefore . . . arm yourselves also with the same attitude" (v. 1). Christ suffered in the flesh and died, therefore we view our lives differently. We count our old life to sin over; the old life, which was dominated by human desires, gives way to the new, courageous life which lives for the will of God (v. 2).

Second, Peter states, "for you have spent enough time" in "wild living" (vv. 3–4). We live according to a new way now, "for" why would a Christian want to live any longer in his old, shameful, lustful, and regrettable ways (v. 3)?

The pagans (meaning unbelieving Gentiles) live this way. Peter lists six of their old ways (v. 3), which are still often celebrated in our world today. They had been living in: first, debauchery, which is unrestrained, shameful living; second, lust, the following of ungodly passions and desires; third, drunkenness, the drinking of large quantities of wine; fourth, orgies, which are wild and immoral parties; fifth, carousing, which again refers to binge-drinking gatherings; and sixth, detestable idolatry, the chief sin of Scripture which leads to countless other sins (see Romans 1:20–23).

Christians are those who have said, "Enough!" to such ways (1 Peter 4:3). Sometimes, when Christians refrain from evil or refuse to endorse what the world says is good, the world will abuse Christians for their restraint (v. 4).

Third, Peter uses the word "but" (v. 5) to bring us back to the truth. Some people live in unrestrained ways, "but" all who ignore or oppose God their Judge will have to answer to Him (v. 6).

Verse 6 is a difficult verse, but it seems to be saying that though the people of God were judged and even killed according to the flesh (e.g., the stoning of Stephen in Acts 7:54–60), yet to God they are now and forever alive. The gospel brought them to eternal life, and now they are not dead to God, but in His presence—they "live according to God in regard to the spirit" (v. 6).

People might judge you unfairly for what they dislike about you now, but God will rescue you, just as He rescued those who have gone before us to be with Him. Hold on!

Are there practical ways you could regularly remind yourself that your new life leaves no place for old sinful ways?

Are you prepared to suffer for doing right? How might you and your church better "arm yourselves with the same attitude" as Christ (1 Peter 4:1) and live "for the will of God" (v. 2)?

Day 24

Read 1 Peter 4:7–11

If my children are struggling with a task, they like to know that the end is in sight. Marathon runners push through pain when the finish line comes into view. Sporting teams tend to score a disproportionate number of points when there are only a few minutes left on the clock. So too, Christians are at their best when they sense that God's delivery on His promises is not far away. It's only a matter of time!

Today's passage begins with: "The end of all things is near" (1 Peter 4:7). Peter is not insisting that Christ would return in his lifetime, or even in the first century. Rather, he is repeating Jesus' teaching that Christians be ever-ready for His return (see Matthew 24:44; Luke 12:35–48).

Much of God's salvation plan in Christ has already been accomplished through Israel's history and the Messiah's life, death, and resurrection. We live in the last privileged days between Jesus' first and second coming. From God's point of view, we're almost there!

In light of that, we can draw strength to finish our race well. So how can we do that? In 1 Peter 4:7, Peter once again urges sober-mindedness and behaviour which stimulates prayer. For example, as we saw in 3:7, a husband's treatment of his wife is

to be such that his prayers are not hindered. A Christian's mind is to be sharply focused on the promises of God, for the sake of our prayers. It seems very important that we live in a way that generates prayer.

As Peter returns to sober-mindedness and prayer, so also he returns to love (see 1:22; 2:17; 3:8). **Peter does not want us to miss the most important things. "Above all, love each other deeply" (4:8).**

I have heard Christians say: "God tells me to love people at church, but I don't have to like them!" But this seems a convenient excuse to not fully embrace those we find difficult to love. At times, a Christian or church elder will need to humbly confront sinful behaviour, as Jesus and Paul teach. Some behaviour needs to be confronted and repentance may be needed for restored fellowship (see Matthew 18:15–17; 1 Corinthians 5). Yet, usually in church life, love allows Christians to show grace to one another instead of holding grudges or breaking fellowship, as "love covers over a multitude of sins" (1 Peter 4:8).

We might then ask: "But how are we to love people deeply?" Peter directs us to focus on serving one another. Those with housing and food willingly share that form of God's kindness (v. 9); those who teach and preach pass on truths they themselves undeservedly received (v. 10); and all who serve carry out their service with the strength God provides (v. 11).

Peter's point is that we love others by serving. And we can serve only because God has first been gracious to us. This kind of loving, humble service glorifies God—"so that in all things God may be praised through Jesus Christ. To him be the glory and the power for ever and ever. Amen" (v. 11).

ThinkThrough

How strong is your sense of the nearness to the glorious end that God has promised?

How might this sense of nearness help you to gratefully love and to actively serve your church family in the coming days?

Day 25

Read 1 Peter 4:12–16

Like many who give their lives to Christ in our world today, the Christians in Peter's day also experienced the heat of hostility from family and from society. Peter says: "Do not be surprised at the fiery ordeal that has come on you" (1 Peter 4:12). It is the first time he mentions fire since chapter 1. In 1:7, he used fire to refer to the trials that test our faith and show us our faith is genuine as we cling to Christ through them.

So, too, fire here refers to the various trials the Christians in Peter's day were facing, which Peter says came to them in many forms (1:6). It included being "insulted" (4:14) and enduring "the sufferings of Christ" (v. 13) in ways normally reserved for criminals (vv. 15–16).

Some Christians feel out of place in their school, university, or workplace because they stand up for Christ and refuse to be unfaithful to Him. For other Christians, their trials for Christ are much worse. I've met Christians who had fled their home country in fear of the parents who raised them— how painful it is to be rejected by your own family! Countless sisters and brothers have spent years in prison, many tortured and mercilessly executed.

We might lament such unjust and cruel treatment, and grieve for ourselves or for others. And we might rejoice that even in these times, God is powerfully guarding our faith in Him (1:5). His Word prepares and directs us so that we stand firm. How will that happen?

First, we can be unsurprised when persecution comes (4:12). Second, we can rejoice when we suffer, because it means we share in Christ's sufferings and will rejoice at His return (v. 13). Such Christ-like suffering is a sign of God's blessing and the Spirit's presence with us (v. 14). Third, though humiliated, we remain unashamed, because we bear Christ's name (v. 16). **Isn't it wonderful to realise that by "the Spirit of glory" (v. 14), we not only endure suffering willingly, but also do so with rejoicing and praise?**

Though we have never seen Christ, we love Him enough to suffer terribly for Him. In His mysterious plan, God uses such suffering to make Christians more closely resemble His faithful, suffering Son. Our next stop? Glory!

You might live in a culture that doesn't persecute Christians, but all Christians carry a cross by carrying burdens or making sacrifices for Jesus. What does this look like for you?

How might you practise the three healthy responses to unjust suffering—to be unsurprised, to rejoice, and to be unashamed?

Read 1 Peter 4:17–19

Raising children with loving discipline is good and important, but it is also hard work. When parents feel like giving up, it can be worth thinking about the much harder alternative—that is, how much harder parents' lives would become if they stopped loving or disciplining their children! Family relationships would break down. Sin and selfishness would be unrestrained and quickly compound. Generally speaking, good parenting is the far easier alternative in the long run—the path of much less misery.

Similarly, when we feel like giving up in following Christ, Peter encourages us to think about the alternative. We often struggle now as God's chosen people living away from our promised land, but the alternative of rejecting Christ and His rule brings far worse consequences.

Jesus gave the same assurance about taking the narrow, more difficult path of following Him: "Enter by the narrow gate. For the gate is wide and the way is easy that leads to destruction, and those who enter by it are many. For the gate is narrow *and the way is hard* that leads to life, and those who find it are few" (Matthew 7:13–14, ESV).

Many Christians feel the bruises and scratches of the narrow path that leads to life. **We are saved and we persevere by God's grace, yet the path of Jesus is both worthwhile and hard.**

In God's wise and mysterious plan, we experience the pain now of being exiles in a world not our own. Living in a broken world hostile to God, we sometimes endure difficult treatment, just as our Lord Jesus did. In this way, as Peter says, "it is time for judgment to begin with God's household" (1 Peter 4:17). And yet, Peter also says: "If it begins with us, what will the outcome be for those who do not obey the gospel of God?" In verse 18, he points to Proverbs 11:31 to make this point—if God's way is hard, how much harder must the other way be? If God's friends suffer, how much worse will it be for those who spurn Him?

You might enjoy reading the many examples God gives us in Hebrews 11 of those who wisely trusted God through suffering. Because God is just, time will show that God's ways are best by far. Justice will prevail. God will vindicate himself and His people.

For believers, this earth is as close to hell as we will get. Sadly, for unbelievers, unless they come to Jesus, this world is as close to heaven as they will get. Peter concludes this section with the simple instruction to keep entrusting our soul to our faithful Creator and to press on with doing good (1 Peter 4:19). God has everything very much under control.

ThinkThrough

Can you think of ways you have been disciplined by God?

How might you do good and bring the gospel to someone not yet reconciled to God?

Day 27

You might think that your church is quite ordinary, and that nothing overly impressive or important takes place there. But Peter helps us to see that our churches, led by faithful under-shepherds, are the way the risen Lord Jesus is now leading us to our eternal home with Him.

In John 21:15–17, Jesus charged Peter with the care of His sheep. Here in 1 Peter 5, we see Peter charging his fellow elders to "shepherd" the Chief Shepherd's sheep through their difficult times (vv. 2, 4).

Peter was such a prominent apostle, yet he humbly identifies himself as "a fellow elder" and "a witness of Christ's sufferings" (v. 1). It's a sober view of himself which he encourages other elders to learn from—to be humble and cross-oriented.

At the same time, Peter wants the elders to know that their service of Christ ends with a glory beyond us. He begins and ends his appeal by reminding them of the certain glory ahead (vv. 1, 4); he wants glory with Christ to fill their horizon, to captivate them, and to motivate their faithful service.

How are elders to view their service? It is both a privilege and a responsibility. **If we are elders, we are to see our role as shepherds—not merely leaders or teachers, but followers of the Good Shepherd who lay down our lives for His sheep.** The flock does not belong to the minister or elders—the church is *"God's flock"* (v. 2). The flock is not under the minister's or elders' control, but under their care (v. 2).

The style of Christian leadership is also important. Christian leaders should not "lord it over" the flock, like a boss or school principal who might rule by reminding subordinates of their place. Pastors are not to treat church members or junior staff as inferior servants. Rather, they model to the flock what it means to serve by genuinely serving them. In this way, the most faithful leader is also the most Christ-like servant, whether caring for a flock of 30 or 3,000. Our example, and not just our teaching, is to help people love our Lord who is gentle and humble in heart (see Matthew 11:29).

This is a word not only for pastors and elders, but it is also helpful for churches to know what Scripture requires of Christ's under-shepherds when it comes to appointing pastors and elders. Churches are to look for loving, sacrificial servants who point people to the Good Shepherd and to His glorious gospel of grace. Their role is not to hold elders to account, but to submit to them, as Peter will explain in tomorrow's reading.

Christ continues to love and guide us by providing elders to humbly lead us in His ways. Why not thank God and pray for those who have had this role in your life?

How might you apply some of these principles of Christian servant leadership to the way you serve others in your church?

Day 28

Read 1 Peter 5:5–7

Have you ever met teenagers or young adults who seem wonderfully receptive to God's Word and to learning from their church family? They seem to sincerely respect their elders, and are good listeners. They carefully form their own views about God's Word, and yet realise they have so much to learn. They are quick to admit their shortcomings, and seem so grateful for God's grace. In a word, they have humility.

Whatever your age, how humble are you? How might you grow in humility?

Throughout Scripture, God seems to particularly bless the humble. The Law fostered humility by demanding that sin be regularly acknowledged through guilt offerings. The Prophets, Psalms, and Wisdom literature commended humility as a trait of the wise (see Isaiah 5:21; Psalm 18:27–30; Proverbs 1:5–7). And Jesus stressed the importance of humility by bringing healing to the humble who realised they were spiritually sick, rather than to those who considered themselves healthy; He calls sinners rather than the self-righteous (Matthew 9:12–13).

Having called elders to humbly shepherd the flock (1 Peter 5:1–4), in today's reading Peter speaks to the young before addressing the whole church. What is the special message for the young? The young are to humbly submit to their elders (v. 5).

Peter's whole letter has urged all of us to be humble and submissive— in society, in the home, in the workplace, and in the church. A humble flock makes the elders' role much easier, and is essential for church harmony. With humility comes mutual growth and deep, loving friendships. Our church elders will make mistakes, and may not do things the way we think best, but these are the leaders God has provided to care for us.

When you get dressed each morning, why not recite 1 Peter 5:5: "All of you, clothe yourselves with humility towards one another, because, 'God opposes the proud but shows favour to the humble.'" **Whatever your clothes, don't forget to wear humility. In God's economy, humility benefits us and makes us more like Jesus, the greatest servant of all.** The alternative is toxic human pride, but God and pride don't mix well.

We might be reluctant to submit to others if we are worried about the consequences. Peter seems to sense this by following yet another call to humility with an assurance: "Humble yourselves, therefore, under God's mighty hand, that he may lift you up in due time. Cast all your anxiety on him because he cares for you" (vv. 6–7)

God's care is not just emotional caring, but He is actually taking care of us. You can trust Him with all your anxiety! It takes a humble confidence in God for us to do that, but He blesses and relieves us as we do.

Some Christians cast their anxieties on God by writing in a prayer journal daily or praying in a small group. How might you develop the habit of daily casting all your anxieties on the mighty God who cares for you?

How would life be different for you if you cast your anxieties on God more regularly?

Read 1 Peter 5:8–11

In many places, pilots are not permitted to fly a plane if they have consumed alcohol in the last 8 or 12 hours. Ideally, there should be no alcohol in the pilot's system at all while responsible for so many lives.

Peter considers a sober mind to be so important that he promotes it repeatedly (see 1 Peter 1:13; 4:7). He even closes his letter by saying it one last time: "Be alert and of sober mind" (5:8).

An alert and sober mind does not seem to be sought after as much as it should be in Christian circles. I am not saying that Christians should abstain from all alcohol, although some choose to do that. Peter is urging Christians to have their minds and vision sharpened by Scripture. Such Christians are wonderfully helpful servants in our churches.

Some might equate being a sober-minded Christian to being a person who has gone to church for many years. But that would be a false equation. **Sober-minded Christians are alert to dangers such as pride, temptation, sexual sin, church factions, false teaching, and greed.** They understand the church's deep need for the grace of Christ as known in the gospel. They don't get carried away by the latest teachings or newest strategies if these seem opposed to the ways of Jesus. They love the Lord Jesus, His people, and the lost, and they have a way of keeping "the main thing" the main thing.

An alert and sober driver will more likely notice dangers ahead, such as a drunk driver or a child running across the road. But the importance of Peter's message is far greater than a road safety message. Peter says there are real spiritual forces at play.

The devil, the ancient tempter and deceiver, would like to see us fall. He is prowling around like a roaring lion looking for easy prey (v. 8). We aren't to be afraid of the devil, whose power is limited by God, but we are to deliberately resist him by holding fast to Jesus, even if the spiritual and social forces against us bring terrible suffering (v. 9). We pursue holiness as God's children, and, unlike Adam and Eve, trust God enough to resist the devil's temptations and distractions.

Peter concludes with a wonderfully rich description of "the God of all grace" and His plans for these churches under fire. It summarises the thrust of 1 Peter as a whole: "And the God of all grace, who called you to his eternal glory in Christ, after you have suffered a little while, will himself restore you and make you

strong, firm and steadfast. To him be the power for
ever and ever. Amen" (vv. 10–11).

_____

_____

_____

_____

_____

ThinkThrough

Read 1 Peter 5:10–11
a few times, slowly.
What do these
verses do in your
heart and mind as
you read them?

How can these
verses help you to
be clear-minded
today and into the
future?

_____

_____

_____

_____

_____

_____

_____

_____

_____

_____

_____

_____

_____

_____

_____

Day 30

Many businesses make decisions after doing a cost-benefit analysis. They might ask: "If we were to renovate our office or employ another worker, would the benefits outweigh the costs?" We also make those kind of decisions all the time for ourselves and our families. What is the best path to take with the various options in front of us?

In contexts of persecution like those we read about in 1 Peter, why would anyone decide to follow the Lord Jesus? Why would anyone be baptised into a community of persecuted Christians? And perhaps, you sometimes wonder if following Jesus wholeheartedly is worth the consequences that might follow.

When a friend of mine became a Christian, his parents said to him: "Okay, so you are a Christian. That is disappointing for us. If you must be a Christian, don't take it too seriously. Don't make trouble for your family or give up your family's religion." What should he do?

1 Peter has been written to assure you that Jesus is absolutely worth suffering for. **If you remember just one thing from this devotional, remember what Peter says in 1 Peter 5:12: "I have written to you briefly, encouraging you and** testifying that *this is the true grace of God. Stand fast in it."*

If we were ever to do a cost-benefit analysis, we must remember that the gospel of Jesus is not a man-made religious story, nor is it an optional path among other good options. Peter wants us to share his certainty that "this is the true grace of God" (v. 12).

The God who made the world offers salvation to the world, and this salvation comes in no other way than through the sacrificial death of His Son (see Acts 4:12). There is no other path to God. So-called "prosperity gospels" are tempting but false; moralism looks good but creates proud self-righteousness and Pharisaic judgmentalism. The gospel which Peter shares here is the true grace of God. And so, even when it hurts, we know it is worth standing firm in it.

Lastly, Peter says that he is writing from Babylon, which may be his way of referring to Rome (1 Peter 5:13; see also Revelation 18:10, 21). In the Old Testament, Babylon symbolised opposition to God's rule. In Peter's day, it was the Roman Emperors who persecuted God's people and stood in defiance of God. Peter then makes special mention of Mark, the author of Mark's Gospel, who was probably with him in Rome. It seems Mark learned much about Jesus' life from Peter.

Peter's final words call Christians once again to love one another, and he prays that God's peace will be theirs: "Peace to all of you who are in Christ" (1 Peter 5:14).

ThinkThrough

Look back over 1 Peter. In what different ways has God encouraged you to stand firm in the gospel of Jesus, the true grace of God?

Having finished reading through this powerful and important letter, how has your appreciation for Jesus increased, and what kind of person is God encouraging you to be?

Going Deeper

in Your Walk
with Christ

Whether you're a new Christian or have been a Christian for a while, it's worth taking a journey through the Bible, book by book, to gain a deeper appreciation of who Jesus is and how we can follow Him.

Let faithful Bible teachers be your tour guides and help you draw closer to Christ as you spend time reading and reflecting on His Word.